A Visit From Grandma

Imani S. Howard

Illustrations by
Gil Balbuena Jr.

To order additional copies of this book, contact:
Xlibris LLC
1-888-795-4274
www.Xlibris.com
Orders@Xlibris.com

A Visit From Grandma
Imani S. Howard

Aisha always looked forward to spending summers at her grandmother's farm. What she enjoyed was spending time with the animals. Her grandmother had chickens, cows, pigs, and horses. There was a horse in particular that was her favorite. His name was Smokey. He got his name because his color was gray mixed with just a little bit of black. Aisha had taking a liking to him because her favorite color was gray.

Towards the end of the school year, Aisha became full of excitement. She asked her mother, "Is it almost time to see grandma?" Her mother replied, "Yes dear, it is almost time."

One morning after her mother dropped Aisha off at school, her mother wasn't feeling well and decided to go to the doctor. The doctor told her mother that she would have to stay in the hospital for a while.

Later that afternoon when Aisha had finished her homework, her mother called her down to the kitchen. Aisha yelled from the bedroom, "Be right there mom." When Aisha walked into the kitchen, her mother said, "Aisha I need to talk to you." "What about mom?" Aisha asked. Her mother said, "After I dropped you off at school this morning, I wasn't feeling well and I went to the doctor. The doctor told me I would have to stay in the hospital for a while." "Oh no, Aisha cried, are you going to be all right?" Her mother replied, "Yes honey, I am going to be just fine, but you won't be able to visit grandma this summer. She will be coming here instead."

Her mother expected Aisha to be very upset and disappointed, but was shocked at Aisha's response. Aisha said, "I don't mind. I just want you to get well. Grandma and I will have a great time here in the city. I'll miss Smokey though." "Can I go visit grandma next summer, Mom?" "Yes, you sure can," her mother answered. "When will grandma be here, mom?" Aisha asked. "She will be here at the end of June when school lets out," her mother said. Aisha couldn't wait. The last day of school had finally arrived. Just as Aisha was getting out of the car she asked, "Will grandma be here when I come home from school?" "Yes Aisha, grandma will be here when you get home," her mother said. Aisha couldn't wait until the final bell rang at three. She was very excited about spending the summer in the city with her grandmother.

When Aisha got off the school bus, she saw her grandmother standing on the steps. She was so excited that she dropped her school bag on the ground and ran to her grandmother. "Oh grandma, I am so glad to see you," said Aisha. "I am glad to see you too. Now go back and pick up your bag," her grandmother said.

Although Aisha was glad to see her grandmother, she was sad about her mother going into the hospital. Before she got into bed, she said a small prayer: "Please God, let my mom be okay." Aisha quickly fell into a deep sleep. She rose the next morning to the smell of her grandmother's pancakes. Of all the dishes her grandmother made, this was by far her favorite. As she started downstairs, she heard her mother crying and went into her room. "Why are you crying, mom?" asked Aisha. "I am sad that I'm going to be away from you and grandma," her mother replied. "Don't worry mom, grandma and I are going to be fine," Aisha said.

Aisha and her grandmother stood in the doorway and watched as her mother got into the taxi and drove way. "What would you like to do today?" Aisha's grandmother asked. "Let's go see a movie," Aisha answered. Aisha helped her grandmother wash and put away the dishes and they got ready for the first day out in the city.

The city had changed since her grandmother lived here. The buildings grew taller. There were also more stores and more people then she remembered. As they were walking, they came upon an ice cream shop. "Let's have ice cream before the movie grandma, okay?" asked Aisha. "Okay," her grandmother said. Aisha and her grandmother found a table and shared the biggest banana split Aisha had ever seen. "Wow grandma, this is a lot of ice cream. Do you think we will be able to finish it all?" asked Aisha. "Well Aisha, Whatever we don't finish, we'll take it home and have it for dessert," her grandmother said.

During the movie, Aisha and her grandmother enjoyed popcorn, soda, and hotdogs. "I don't want to take the bus home grandma, can we walk instead?" Aisha asked. "We sure can," said grandma. Over the next few weeks, Aisha and her grandmother did all kinds of things. They visited the park, the museum, the zoo, and they even went on a hayride. Aisha loved being with her grandmother, but she really missed her mother. She hoped she would come home soon. "When is mom coming home?" Aisha asked. "I talked with mom this morning. She said it shouldn't be much longer. The doctor wants to do a few more tests," her grandmother said.

The next morning, Aisha awoke to the sound of rain hitting against the window. She went into her grandmother's room. She saw that her grandmother looked very sad. "What's wrong grandma?" asked Aisha. Her grandmother replied, "I talked to your mother this morning. She didn't want me to wake you. Her grandmother was silent for a moment. Aisha your mother needs to have an operation on her heart." "Is she going to be okay?" Aisha asked. "I don't know," her grandmother said. "Can we go see her today?" asked Aisha. "Yes, but we must have breakfast first," her grandmother answered.

When they got to the hospital, Aisha and her grandmother stopped at the gift shop. "Let's buy mom some flowers grandma," said Aisha. "Okay you pick them Aisha," said her grandmother. Aisha picked a big bouquet of red and blue carnations. "Do you think mom will like them grandma?" Aisha asked. "Yes, Aisha, your mother will love them." replied her grandmother. Her grandmother paid for the flowers, they left the gift shop, and took the elevator to the fifth floor.

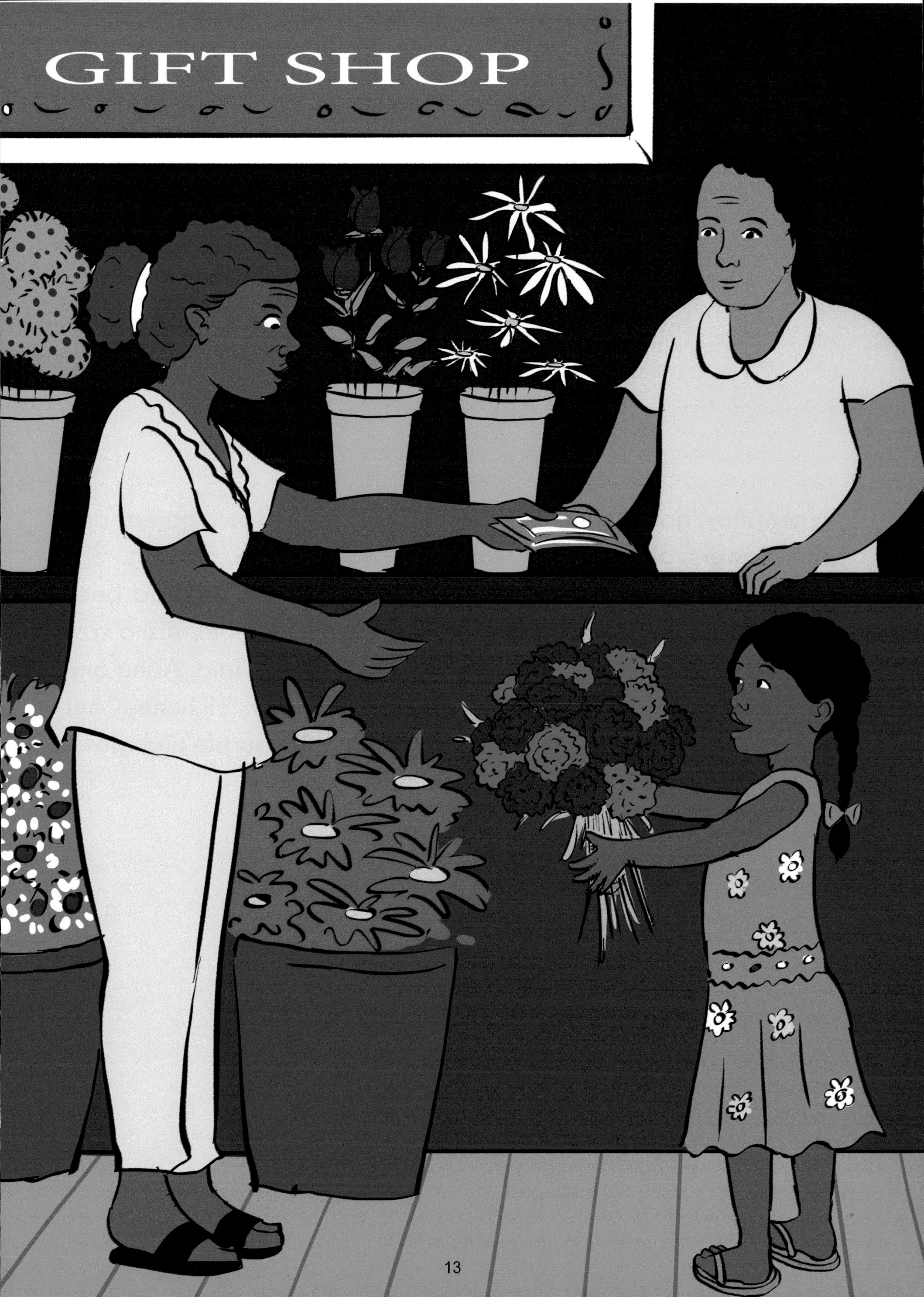
GIFT SHOP

When they got off the elevator, Aisha saw purple, green, and pink flowers all over the walls. She was a little nervous. She had never been in a hospital before. She felt like she had been walking forever. When they got to her mother's room, Aisha saw her mother's name outside the door. "This is it," she said. Aisha and her grandmother walked in. "Hi, mom." Aisha said. "Hi honey," her mother replied. Aisha's mother was wearing the purple nightgown that Aisha had given her last Christmas.

It had been a long time since Aisha and her mother talked. Aisha told her mother about all the things she and her grandmother did. Aisha's mother could only smile at the joy on her daughter's face. "Are they going to make your heart better mom?" Aisha asked. "Yes, Aisha, the doctors are going to do their very best," her mother replied. Aisha and her grandmother stayed and they all had lunch together. Just as they were finishing, the nurse came in to take her mother's temperature. "Where's the bathroom?" Aisha asked. "Let me show you. It's right down the hall," the nurse said. The nurse and Aisha walked out of the room. The doctor walked in. "How soon after the operation will I be able to go home, doctor?" Aisha's mother asked. "If all goes well, you should be able to go home in a week or two," the doctor replied.

When Aisha returned her mother said, "The doctor said I will be able to come home in a couple of weeks. Then you, grandma, and I can spend the rest of the summer together." "That's great!" Aisha replied. When it was time to leave, Aisha and her grandmother kissed Aisha's mother and they all said I love you. The ride home was long. Aisha fell asleep on her grandmother's shoulder. Aisha's grandmother woke her up when the taxi pulled up in front of their house. Once inside, Aisha kissed her grandmother goodnight, went upstairs, and began getting ready for bed.

The next day, Aisha was playing in the back yard when she heard a car pull up. She went to the front door and opened it. She was very excited and surprised to see her mother get out of the taxi. "Mom, I'm so glad you're home," Aisha said. "The doctor said I could leave the hospital early because I was feeling better. I am glad to be home with you and grandma," her mother said.

That evening, Aisha's grandmother made a wonderful welcome home dinner for Aisha's mother. They all had a wonderful time. There were three weeks left until the end of the summer. Aisha, her mother, and her grandmother enjoyed those three weeks together.

Printed in the United States
by Baker & Taylor Publisher Services